THE OLDER GRACES

Also by David Manicom

Poetry
Sense of Season (Press Porcépic, 1989)
Theology of Swallows (Oolichan Books, 1991)

Fiction
Ice in Dark Water (Véhicule, 1997)

The Older Graces

by

David Manicom

OOLICHAN BOOKS
LANTZVILLE, BRITISH COLUMBIA, CANADA
1997

Copyright © 1997 by David Manicom. ALL RIGHTS RESERVED. No part of this publication may be reproduced, stored in a retrieval system, or transmitted, in any form or by any means, without prior written permission of the publisher, except by a reviewer who may quote brief passages in a review to be printed in a newspaper or magazine or broadcast on radio or television; or, in the case of photocopying or other reprographic copying, a licence from CANCOPY (Canadian Copyright Licensing Agency), 6 Adelaide Street East, Suite 900, Toronto, Ontario M5C 1H6

Canadian Cataloguing in Publication Data

    Manicom, David, 1960-
    The older graces

Poems.
ISBN 0-88982-164-X
I. Title.
PS8576.A545O6 1997   C811'.54   C97-910279-0
PR9199.3.M348504 1997

We acknowledge the support of the Canada Council for the Arts for our publishing programme.

THE CANADA COUNCIL | LE CONSEIL DES ARTS
FOR THE ARTS | DU CANADA
SINCE 1957 | DEPUIS 1957

Grateful acknowledgement is also made to the BC Ministry of Tourism, Small Businesss and Culture for their financial support.

Published by
Oolichan Books
P.O. Box 10, Lantzville
British Columbia, Canada
V0R 2H0

Printed in Canada by
Morriss Printing Company Limited
Victoria, British Columbia

for my mother and father

Acknowledgements

I would like to thank Mark Abley, Diana Brebner, George Elliott Clarke, Steven Heighton, and Ron Smith for their support of my work. Their words and advice, at various times and places, were more important than they knew. Natalia Kisselevska verified and corrected my translation of Tsvetaeva. Ambassador Michael Bell and Bella Akhmadulina gave some of these poems an audience in Moscow. Charlie Foran was essential. Teresa read each poem first and helped make it possible to write them.

Some of these poems have previously appeared in *Saturday Night, More Garden Varieties* (Aya Press/The League of Canadian Poets, 1989), *Zymergy, Matrix, Quarry Magazine, Bookware: Ottawa Valley Poetry* (1994), *Vintage 93* (Quarry Press/The League of Canadian Poets, 1994) *Windhorse Reader: Choice Poems of '93* (Samurai Press, 1994) and the *Windhorse* broadsheet, 1996. Special thanks to John Castlebury.

Contents

I
13 Radiation

II
19 Cover Their Faces

III
31 Penates
32 The First Day
33 Domestic
34 Vesuvian
35 Accident With Morning Coffee
36 Livestock
38 The Dreams of Artemis
39 Accidental: One of the Erinyes
41 Lullaby of the Meister
42 Autumn Evening Sees Through the Blindness of Prayer
43 A Lacquered Fan
45 The Well
46 The Swimmer
48 Flyways

49 Mount Elgin in the Fields
50 The Train
51 In the Valleys of Alma-Ata
52 Sex and Work
53 Field
54 Another Life
55 Montréal Love Letter
56 The Voice, Revived
57 The Older Graces

IV
61 Romania

V
73 Why I Need You
75 Ophelia Dreams of Akhmatova
77 To T.M.
78 Histories of Silence
83 October Again, Moscow
84 Notes to the Poems

"In some places the grim Erinyes (or Furies) were closely associated in cult with the benevolent Graces. This combination of the terrible and the benign was frequently found in the character of chthonian deities."

—Edward Tripp

I

Radiation

a Betty Goodwin triptych, for Diana Brebner

I

(The Swimmers)

As if in love you might "burrow into the gesture"—
Their drowning bodies in this revealed transparency
Are not themselves entirely opaque, the torsos starred
Like old lenses and marred within by odd incisions, dust.
The instrument is absent: lust or the painter's brush
And nervous grip. See thus only what is left behind,
Cancerous, the disease nothing of itself, a blind stir,
Its former presence afterward inferred, a door
No one has seen opened by no one passing through
Into the avenue of doors, a swift inanimacy.

You wrote me capering a thinking cap of flesh,
"Our best skinhead poet," a lovely, bragging terror.
I felt the first rift in the fields of gravity.
Now my mother has her hands in water, apron tied.
My father pulls the laces of his workboots tight.
Our crazy neighbour cycles madly after trains.
My lover sighs beneath the heavens in the shower.
Your craftsman double-stitches canvas for an arctic night.
Goodwin dims the studio to ease her unbelief,
The swimmers strain to hover in their painted light.

II

(Seated Figure With Red Angle)

"They are seeking a place to breathe, trying to move out."
In my bereft returning unto you the bodies float
Like notes of piano music in a basement flat,
God's transparencies, a colour wash, the density
Of flesh that is deepest at the skin. Concavity stilled.
The windowsills well daylight on your upper walls
So far as I can see, my phone call never getting through,
Your hand floating into view toward the endless ring,
Lesion of your piano playing silenced, raw umber
Part of ivory. I check and re-check the number.

My pure intentions as an underwater line
Between two continents; but it is signs and passages
To *the outside*—not a salvaged intimacy—
You need from me now. My voice, a wire in the canvas,
The swimmers in their final genius contemplate
As just another self-assuring artifact. Yellow
Of cadmium on my palette still, dialing hopelessly,
Sparely tinging white and gathering about the throat
A thickening frottage of cadmium red.
You resume your music. There are no lines in, or out.

III

(Figure With Chair)

The will, you said, turns "Not in the leaving of traces,
But in using what is left to continue," the will
You said, as an eraser like a season
Worked inside the vigour of your figures, into black clouds
And tailings, brute diagonal strokes as if
Some fundamental chair, the very seat of airs
Tipped slowly, a declension of the word *fear*.
There is thickening at the nape, a collar of war.
Inside, the scraping leaves but shallows of your plans—
Is that another, smaller head, cringing near the heart?

And so the forward pressure, like a purchased debt,
That sense of slippage, of the angles drawn
For the new arrangement of the coat, the toys,
The pillow and the key. Do your hips press forward,
A shoulder turning in the gladed light, eyes lifting
But never quite to bear? The sound of a knife
Scraping dry toast. You? You could rise at night
And find a stranger standing in the shadowed hall,
Not like a dream but as if there are no dreams.

II

"Not just a swerving, but a throwing back,
As if regret were in it and were sacred."

—Robert Frost

Cover Their Faces

(An Ending Placed First)

The dawn my brother reached his porch devoid of dread.
O Christ call out to other hillsides, shred
Your faith again and stagger at our lovely dead . . .

The streamlets, radicals of ocean, plumbed
New Brunswick loam for first faint inspirations
Of earthly water, an endless dendrite gathering

The raw and yet unbearably resolved
Meeting with the world—the night his car turned
Home across the Peticodiac, current

Carrying the great, cool, long-in-building swerve
Down to meet the upstream, coming-at-us wave
Of tidal bore, its counter, awful calm: *Love*

And be silent. Curlews on pearl parchment. Metal pools
And mud flats. Cattail balance. The sea over the hill.

(ii)

He dreamt he stepped into home and awoke within a tomb.

Driving the causeway back from night shift his life cruised
In thoughtless, sea-air, getting to bedness, roused
Into the kitchen-state of half alert where we lose

Much of what comes dear by the back screen door banging
In a damp southness off Shepody Bay, changing
His history. *No seconds? All myself?* Waking.

In the hushed chamber he found and unwrapped her limbs
(You've heard this long ago) the sirens still a dim
And ultramarine future, the rifle, the hammered whim

The murder all gone, out-of-province. Within the house
A faultless dream inside a dream wherein he must
Stare out from windows as the causeway turns to dust.

(iii)

> "My mother left me in the next village
> with a false name pinned to my skirt."

Today, killed sister, when I asked the refugee
Orphaned by Pol Pot about her siblings, so softly
That I leaned to her she said, "Seven, now just me."

Then, "what is, refugee?" I stuttered, pointed—You.
And so your pain: the unsymbolic residue
Of *breathing easily*, without referral *of* or *to*.

Behind the outward surge of heart, our swale, our lee,

Sweet hut in night woods, sleek craft on open bay;
But as frontier and inner bleed, as foreknown memory,
Hurt: writing on the inner wall, brain wire, key

Only to the passage further in, where in the end
Again the body, room filling with smoke, and the final dream
Of a dove grey glove turned inside out at dawn.

(iv)

We fled dawn and drove across the flats of day
Deeply into walled night, a family flayed
Funnelling from Toronto, the North, the Outaouais

Meeting like the rivers of Ontario near Montreal,
A current through the long, St. Lawrence, tensely cheerful
Afternoon, a winding of cars, buoyed by the needful,

Turning south into evening at Rivière du Loup,
All elemental travellers now, adept at passing through,
Curving down New Brunswick in our threading row,

Taillights, past midnight, the mind by itself. Suddenly

We had ravelled a nightmare umbilicus: we were there.
Those who had come before us now at last appeared
Moving slowly through the porchlight to greet the cars.

(v)

We passed the kleenex boxes to the next seized need
Like collection baskets back and up the row, fists freed
By this small service, and I thought *Had he panicked?*

Gun-panicked as if his heart throbbed in his hands.

We sang the psalms as if trying to raise a flag,
And I thought of cleansers and the kitchen rags
The man had used on walls and bloody rugs.

My hand shifted on my knee, a crouching bird.
Blinking I was caught where he gagged, then slowly strolled
Without hope down the sloped corridor of his mind.

She's dead as earth. Outside, each tie of love unknots.
The camera crews, like children, stared from the parking lot.
"Suffer them all to come," He said, but I could not.

(vi)

That long nightfall I stalked my sleeping child
Through the inside-outable room as grandma called and called
Into the autumn coal chute years above my head

Where I plunged down the hoof-pocked outhouse hill
From her sofa-by-the-cookstove life, faster until my will
Left me and pushed from behind as part of the world,

The thief robbed in his bed, the king with a kopeck
Begging in the underpass realm, my neck
Bare to the air, my arms wide with being six

Through the old elbowy orchard and trippy grass,

Lifting my four-year-old back from the edge,
Grandma waving my scarf and hat from the top of the path
Calling "Landsakes sweetheart, you'll catch your death."

(vii)

Then too, water turned unnoticed into wine.
The feast of marriage at the bride's was kitchen
Music, nook and cranny chairs set out to *eat*, not dine—

Yes, the same house, same linoleum, same wood—
Dishes in the rack, coats thrown in on the bed,
Paper tablecloths and plates, beer and bread

And the great lobster-crammed hamper on the counter

Brought on ice at noon from the sea at Shediac
For eating cold, and we from an inland foreign state
Grappling with rosy shells. With patient probes and chat

They showed the slow extraction of the sweetest meats.
We drove back happy with the groom across the tidal flats
And slept beneath his eaves in Riverview.

(viii)

> "*The most misleading sign was the skeletal*
> *survivors on their cots*"

"Love, I see you at the window and the road's lone light—"
Weary, what you cannot think of is my absent thought—
"Your breath blossoming on glass—" *What you sought*

Was my past voice, your necessary imagination,
Not for creation and the mind's ascension
"—Sea, seaglass, a single kill—" *just desperation*

The common art, figures of a reflex blind and bound
In its hot closet of grief, lashing to envision
My attention, salvation into pain, the flinch again

And the inner life— "It is all recorded, kept—"

I used to tell you, we are living, let it pass—
"I have not been fooled—" *This is not my voice—*
Gun, nape, shit, roar, blood, silence. The swim across.

(ix)

So we chatted quietly beneath the moon
At one a.m., not tired now, did the rounds
Of introductions, normally. My brother's wounds

Were each insane, and it took time to learn
Their language of ridiculous speech. He went among
Us. Then I remember looking for him, and my father,

And saw them suddenly, alone and broken free

Into the lost, suspended, external space
Of one another's male, unhoused arms, faces
Still unfacing the unused love between, away

From where the rest of us still clustered at the cars.
Each stood like Cordelia holding onto Lear,
Each held a father with a child's fear.

(x)

Of all things soft and gathered in the dark,
All edgeless densenesses for which the mind embarks
In honour of its own infolded, covert-

Even-to-itself foundations, clearly contained
Yet undimensioned, sweet peace of a bed
In winter covers, clothes closet for a child,

Hayloft rich with dust and slanted sun—
But here the large breath of trees; and the river runs
As a bar of light below ripe slopes of corn.

Reduced and ordered to our groupings on these lawns—

Ashes in a little box afloat in earth.
It was just the size for gloves, and so I treasure her
Grey and soft and gathered, laid within, unpaired.

III

"Je bois près de ta soif."

—Yves Bonnefoy

Penates

I came to the farm just before morning.
Here is where hills are hulls of greater ships
That can move this slowly, preserving weather.
The dead lie on their decks with loam faces
And broken attitudes watching erasure
Of eyelids and the fine rigging of roots.
Here the wind is a deep current, cold, brutal
With the scents of season and forced breath.
When we were children I hid in the porch
—the laths! coarse against my cheek—
And watched mother stay out in the garden
Long after dark, tending its colourless petals
With the faint Morse of her shears. At last
Her shadow split from the columns of trees

And passed, hiding its face, red eyes turned
To the empty, intimate pastures.
Now I've become where all aversions stare.
Here is where love is kept and cannot escape.
What I was blind to, in this place is vision,
Where the hulls, where the sheer fissures of sail—
Here I am free only to remain.

The First Day

> *(a translation of "Le Premier jour"*
> *by Marie-Claire Blais)*

At the hour I passed through the doorway
No one was speaking in the rooms of our house—
Someone had tenderly closed each of the doors
And the hearts were holding their silence,
The humid, heavy life was sliding
Mysteriously between my arms—
It was not long after a little party,
I was listening to the sonorous birthday
Of the earth travelling between my arms,
And the others lay as still in the fields
As the windrows, and laboured no more.

It lasted no more than an instant.
At the table they were waiting for bread,
They had left their fragile souls on the floor,
Their love was becoming no more than themselves
In the drying of spring into summer—
No one spoke through the rooms of our house—
The tranquil horses of evening
Appeared no more in the road—
Someone had veiled the windows with sheets
And somewhere there in the hovering dust
They listened to the first of my crying.

Domestic

Outside in the timely shadows
Of the silo, in the cow-less
Cowyard's deep remissness and dry
Dungsoil—(the place *knows* me; mind
The opened metal bed
Of the watertank, its red float
And cold dirty drink, its remote
Rippling sky; and I hope still
Almost luminous in the housely
Shade the blue licking blocks of salt
Carved into cups and beautifully damp
Henry Moores by the soothed, consuming tongues).

Vesuvian

Night heat stronger than our cursive fears
Sprawled us here straight as death on our bed.

The television light soundlessly fingered
The chalky, lingering casts of our sex.

Curtains expectant as the countryside eased;
A slight breeze chilled the furled cotton sheets.

The black grass. The tired thickets of leaves.
Sleeves of the shadows. Mute insect drifts.

The back screen door tapped against the jamb,
A colourless slow river crossed. Like flotsam

Small hearts carried inward until clipped
To the crosswires. If I slip to the right room

Are we still there like two bones in blue light,
Perfect model of our late love, too hot to move?

Accident With Morning Coffee

Alone, I grew careless.
For a few days the deep burn
Removed half of one fingerprint,
Though this is not recorded
In the files of External Affairs;
A taut, silverish crescent
Polished where the flame bit
As water bearing a surface light.
The graven whorls approach and cease
Like you, my love, stepping
From the white, salt-lavished
Timbers of that Gaspé dock
Hugging your horrors of me
Like a leather suitcase
Filled with gravel. Each groove
And loop dies at the smooth glare
As again I see you stepping free,
Allowing me for a moment
The blonde sea grass of your hair
Swimming up as you descend.

An accurate passport snap,
Nine fingers, a gulping heart
With its various natural songs.
And look,
I have imagined your entire life
The razing of a tenth of mine.
I have sung you on one fingertip.
That, I've lost. Think how utterly
The rest of you defines me.

Livestock

(... don't ever write to me again ...)

Tonight while something dark is forgetting me
As gravity will pinch a water droplet
Free, I am colonized with remembering,
Unspared the selling-off when I was six
Fidgeting at father's knees in the mill of crowd
That ground away a neighbour's properties
Lock, Stock and Barrel, as the notice went.
He stooped to swing me to his shoulders,
My boot heels tapping at his coveralls
As the auctioneer began to hammer
Bids into the ring of farmers. They scratched
And nodded, shifted pipes. The neighbours' names
Are gone from me; everyone we knew was there.
Machinery hunkered in the yards
And by the house like art, socks of a drill
Prodding down their snouts, crimpers and
Beached ploughs, scoured wagons with bolted racks
Tilting and groaning in rainy wind. Later
The cows were paraded, their profound bodies
Surging in the striped light of barns,
Tapped behind the knee to make them trot,
Cane-rapped on a shoulder and a hip,
Knocks returning from their velvet hides.
The black metal of the piston voice ...

                    An hour: finished.
Farmers filed to their trucks, the yards
Done to mud. A man shook hands, talked too loud,
A woman gazed from the farmhouse window
As we went in. They had set up a till
On the kitchen table. A kettle bobbled
On its cherry coil, the floral patterns
On the walls spun on and on; she still stands
Facing outward while forgotten hands
Scrub vegetables beneath a running tap.
Dad, I wondered, what are we doing here?
Paying for the rake. We joined a shuffling line.
We'd made a purchase. I hadn't known.
The awakening after one of the deaths.
Hands. In cold water. Tonight
She is rinsing the features from my face.

The Dreams of Artemis

When my beauty is touched there is a payment.
Sometimes I will sluice the children into air
Too soon—a Protestant knee to a Catholic womb
Will do, or I'll slice an appendix like a purse—
So that the parents might watch them gape and die,
Or flail and live. Oddly, either works.
Sometimes I will have the Sabine women raped.
Sometimes I enlist Chilean soldiers
With gasoline and matches; they will take down
Some of the destabilizing eyes
And their company of tiny paintbrushes
And ankle wings. Occasionally
I just turn off minor hearts in their cribs.
I walk through the membrane and revisit love.
A body writhes inside an envelope
Of fumes, flames slowly cool until they freeze,
The surgeons recompose a bulky, plastic face
That has fewer expressions than before.

Accidental

(One of the Erinyes)

From here in the province of humus on wood

I've spirited you where your scream was needed.
That vacation too, has failed. In this maple chair
Of your kitchen bastion I'm waiting through
September with you, plague in the leaves, a tine
Of your voice and its consumption, the pith
Of dried sticks and spurning cloud of jasmin

Flooding the clear water—I don't relent.
You thought from an old world island's mist on stone
The better envelope of your innocence
Might be addressed? But I do not hope
For innocence, and *I* was guide west
Toward the listing, Protestant fields.

Near a holy well's sadistic drip you leaned
Your bike into the cloud of a hedge, dipped
Your wrist in the saint; past a ghost of wall hiked
Higher over the inlaid slabs of the island's
Nature. Your mind began to circle
Like slow oxen or Christian weather,

Walked the blurred outer rings of vast defence,
Embroidered a path through the spiked rocks
Of cheveaux de frise to the capacious
Walls of the fort, nests of clacking, mortarless,
Gathered and unfitted, a scree of your darkness;
Entered the centre's platter of turf, pleasant

Ground save that it gave a lip onto the surf
And three hundred feet of open sound
Hushing and crying and hushing and
Crying, sweater netted with mist, watching the foam,
With the casual cliff across his throat,
Closing the stare in the submarine realm

Of your roaming happy baby glimpsed
Atop the flights of stairs an instant alone
Giggling at air on her bruiseless, prescient skin.
You remembered your bike in the blushing lair
Of the fuchsia, stepped onto gravity
All the way back. I always let you come home.

In the swelling lung of light I watch maxilla,
I'm in your kitchen with my pots of tea
Waiting you out in this sort of world of mine
Where the kitten you let out does not return
And at six downstairs in the dim mailbox
You find a letter for the previous tenant

Waiting for you like a pale hand.

Lullaby of the Meister

Wristwatch on a wooden stool,
Glasses on a face-down book.
Plucked rubber band: the bullfrogs' stout
Insistence. The rest of you dark.

The cause of the watch is death,
The cause of the stool descent,
The cause of the glasses amnesia,
The root of the book, regret.

A breathless insomnious summer,
My heart drops stones in a dry pond.
In the dream which I inhabit
Everyone else is asleep.

I can love your wristwatch,
Your glasses, love
Your face-down book. *Husk*.
I am this lonely.

Autumn Evening Sees Through the Blindness of Prayer

Attached to parched darkness by a throat
The iron stove at night is like a brain.
I seem to sit willingly in *this* quiet.
Logs shift in the muttering stove, flame
Returns from where it has been folded
Down: a sudden animal of air, heart
Of the room. Somewhere limbs tilt, snag, hold—
A meteor scrapes the lake-thinned sky. I start,
Into sleep? Leg slips, swallowed oxygen flees
Into smoke where charred and jewelled lovers
Tense. Tied by cord to what I cannot see
I list upward waiting for the stirring lover
—shadowed by my stare's direction—to move me,
Start the superb stutter of need, flue's roar.

A Lacquered Fan

End of the slow hall ajar, an elbow of light,
I gleaned when I opened spread from the folded
Livings that wind addled the calm butterflies
On a raised window's curtain, and your eyes opened
On surprises of another, snapdragon place,
Leaving me. On the Rorschach table-lace a tin
With a tighter lid, and within a palm's worth
Of richly dusty tea. Let me give birth in hot
Containment. Nightly I have not pried the lid,

Still closed within our precious adjoining rooms,
Have not dredged the moonlit water by your boardwalk
Romanticism; I have not stalked and lifted
The faintly striped and drooping hood to find Jack
In the aquariums of ripe spring wood among
The one-inch maples, a supple green thermometer
In his pulpit. A shudder by seasonal ponds
Under the brittle wands of dry weeds; my watched hands,
Clenched on tabletops, cannot dispel themselves

To drop the two stones I seem to have carried
Out of the old quarry to ripple the long pause
After your last words to me—all sink to the kitchen's
tea-leaf and table-lace and butterfly past.
I lean waiting on moss and lichen stumps to plunge
My fist into the wet lung of your new life room
Where you decay into my forest floor, and pull
Mourning the salamander free, black and quick
As myself in the sheets of the wood-light.

I still own the stones I threw at your silence-
Mirror. I wait by the silver tin unable
To find you anywhere, afraid to jar the rooms
With the shouting lunge that will burst my last
Holding. You are absent even in the dark. Your nights
Have become a hill, and stand-ins have arrived
In my inner tales. If I no longer transfigure
In your nightmare I'm lost beyond my own corings,
Alone under the paling, properly awake.

The Well

(a translation of "Le Puits," by Yves Bonnefoy)

You hear the chain scraping the rock face
When the bucket descends in the well that is the other star,
At times the evening star that comes alone,
At times the undivided fire awaiting dawn
For the beasts and shepherd to emerge.

But always the water is shut in the well's deep,
The star that abides there is always sealed.
Shadows can be distinguished beneath the boughs,
Travellers who are passing through the night,

Stooped, their backs burdened by a dark mass—
Hesitating, it appears, where the paths diverge.
Some seem to wait, others to obscure themselves
In the glittering that proceeds without light.

The journey of a man, a woman, is long, longer than life,
A star at the end of the road, a sky
We once believed we saw shining between two trees.
When the bucket touches the water, and is buoyed,
There is the joy that the chain overwhelms.

The Swimmer

(a translation of "Le Nageur" by Philippe Soupault)

A thousand bird cries,
a lifeline horizon,
vague lost faces
whispering in bays
held open like arms.
At last I'm convinced
I've been left alone
facing west? facing north?
the sun humming down light,
a street of heaven and earth.
I pause to rediscover
that summer is red in my veins
while my shadow sweeps slowly around me
like hands on the face of a clock.
Sleep brings reptiles and insects,
pain, a grimace, a lie,
an awakening.
My face floats lost in the hour
beyond justice or shouts from the shore—
I wander the unending staircase
without convictions or guilt
all the way down into sleep.
In eyes, in mirrors, in wind laugh
I recognized a stranger I am.
I don't move. I wait,

then close the eyes
like a bolt in a lock.
We will never know
when night is about to start
or where it will stop,
but does it all matter
in the final addition?
The blacks of Kamchatka
will drowse beside me tonight
when weariness sits on my head like a crown.

Flyways

I loved you most the first cold day in September.
Toward dusk the rabbits ascended to nibble the weather.
The swings kicked the wind in the emptying park
As if invisible children pumping up
Through this earlier dark of fall had dangled free
Climbing an arc, rising, all that is easily lost.
The delicate slides stood prehistorically still.

Above us a river of starlings surged and blossomed,
Spanning the sky with a body of infinite parts,
Tracking the Ottawa south, riding and cutting the gusts;
Yet within, a turmoil of individual flight,
And, when it passed, a chaff of stray birds
Blown in the heavens. I linked small fists to each hand
And headed for home, as well as I could.

Mount Elgin in the Fields

I.M. Hazel Manicom, 1908-91

Behind these trees silvered by impending storm, the fields.
The *mount* hardly a hill, a rise in the highway
Poised slightly apart from the farms. Today your hearse
Purred respectfully slowly in climbing, barely
Surpassing tractors wagoning barley. And now
It's not much of a village. Both churches fallow,
A post office rationed then shut, and the low wooden stage
Where I gazed into meadows of Methodist angels
At Sunday School pageants collapsed from the lack of our weight.
Undusted, innate, a canvas Hosanna still hovers
In rafters. The general store's rattling *Fanta*
Is rust. Grandma, your children, your scores of relations,

Came down from the crest to the grave in coloured
Knots of reunion, wind in their dresses and pant cuffs,
Wind in their eyes. The yearning of *Softly and Tenderly*
Followed like sunshine and gale from the funeral:
We all longed to want Jesus. From where you now lie,
By a husband these twenty years dead—we remembered
Forgetting—Mount Elgin slopes to an autumn's
Shaved hillsides and ploughing, where next summer again
The barley will surge in each gust like a muscular pelt,
So that here you could kneel and watch over gradual fields
(Were you anything else but the fields).

The Train

In your fist a bolt of colour, in my words

The wheels of your trains roll off, come unbound
Like the refugee pearls of a necklace snapped
From the neck; the thick purple crayon
Of your smoke zeds to the foot of the page
In defiance of natural law, downcast
And drained; the teetering stack of your tracks
Runs up out of reach; the box cars are rhomboids
That butt and abut like battering males
Of the species; faces at windows are X's
Blue and blinded with care; and the cowcatcher
Floats from the front above the gaze of the crowd,
A comb with its orange teeth ablaze,
Ready to spear the cattle that jump at the moon
In a world we can only witness combined:

Three and colouring; thirty three, scared.
But a very real place. (I love you, there.)

In the Valleys of Alma-Ata

I cannot sleep, two hundred miles from China,
Without your cupped hips and two forests of hair,
The cool prow of your back where I pull toward night
On the delicate dream craft we daily repair.

The satellites circle with slow, canting mirrors
Above the cold peaks of the western Tien-Shan,
The leopards, the wheat fields of all Kazakhstan,
Alone in the darkness, like two human hands

Which cannot rest, two hundred miles from China,
Far from the currents our murmurings steer,
Where we turn in unison without ever waking
On the delicate dream craft we daily repair.

Sex and Work

There is the cool glass bowl with weighted fruit—
You, relaxed and yet astute. Have you not wished
To rest thus hushed and poised habitually,
Subtly composed and yet distinct? Breakfast,
Sunlight, Mozart. Apples, lime, and the last
Suede peach. This was for the opening lines,
Not for our years of finding out our love
Exactly as our lives, burnt with sex and work.
I saw it, shaken, on a hotel balcony,
Stung by beauty in an unfamiliar town's

Summer night-wind, beat and high with jet lag,
The city lights like embers on a blackened log.

Field

Her cool hand; milkweed;
    a curious sheath;
An outer shell of seed;
The silk under seed.

Another Life

I ran from the suitable house at morning
Pulling my conscious collar against forlorn weather
Down the caressive lanes, leather and wool dream,
To find him, warm with half-wild foliage and breath
Under the dawn rain's cellar light, impelled, divined.

Is that what a father is, that I found your sleep
In a cottage land deep with hedgerows, blue flags swept,
The quilt clean; and somehow rags, work-thin and stained,
Only in the end, wrapped roughly on your singular
And too familiar limbs, so untended, lapsed?

And you a white horror lunging a last wish
That I go and leave you there, a wraith famished
In this room by each desire I learned nothing of,
Now in your landscapes like three lifting doves, like quilts
Hung out on mist and apple trees, unsilted love.

Did I tell you of the winter evenings, hunting bread—
We pressed past flower sellers led by perfect laws
To guard their roses against the frost
In glass and wooden cases warmed by candlelight—
The metro's nightly reliquaries, hearts gone forth?

No. Now you pace like my private convict
Pale and bodiless on unwatched screens, relentless
In your basement rooms, as if coming to your deathbed
Were not dreamed too late, the marriage quilts unaired,
As if you come to seek asylum even here.

Montréal Love Letter

Each day of our love deserved a moment of dread.
The nebular streetlights through afternoon curtains
Of snow squalls and darkness on *rue Esplanade*;
Hanging their heads down, afoot in the whipping of drifts.
Wistful *balcons* and the shifting of hollows,
Handwritten S's of snow hard by the houses,
The buses that lumbered clear from the static
As visions of rest. I wished you my heart in this shape:
An accordion wrestled with air in the nest
Of the storm, its surges redressing the prairie
Convictions of wind through the muscle of music
In the crook of the invisible blind man, barely awake
In his vests as he played for coins on *St-Viateur*.
Behind the white foliage of cold, his bus-stop laments
Bodily loomed.
Figures turn and return under flannelette sheets.
The skeins of his notes were tightening wires,
A rachet of airs. *Mons pays ce n'est pas
Un pays* it's an accordion played in the snow.
The wind as it slackened to heavier falls
Lifted the sidewalks and lowered the clouds.
A pointillist evening
Half-lit and sifting, a slow deflation of sound
As the city re-entered the fragile cinema realm.
Walked-out at last, I came to our flat from the corner
Booting through powdery waves, peering through breath
And longing for light in the second floor window; saw
The delicate drifts lie around me like pale violins,
Heard an accordion song like a fence in the blizzard.

The Voice, Revived

(a translation of "La voix, qui a repris," by Yves Bonnefoy)

"Have you come through need of this place,
Of this place alone, its ravine, its door hung
Above the rising up and lying down
As passes the boat of another world—
Come in: I permit you, almost, a resting place.

Have you come here, at least this once,
To be master of the threshold, to press the weight
Of the studded door on its sleeping hinge
And trouble this dream, knowing too well
That each threshold is a dream, and this iron
The undeniable sign, yet with no promises—
I permit you the key in the heavy door.

Have you come to hear the echoes
Of hammers under the vaulted roofs
Even now retreating, fading, seeing
The light but in dreams, descending
With eyes full of tears toward the sky
That welcomed you from yard to yard
Among the almond trees and clear oaks—
Look. I will have given you, in the retaking,
A native earth, and there is nothing else."

The Older Graces

"The words are aching in their own pursuit."
                              —Derek Mahon

Having lived in heaven I am here,
A hooded man, my fingers singing *Where*
In tenor light, a casting into air
From tree to island tree. To pure warp
Of harpstrings I imagined weft, the weir
Of lifted water, fishnet, am left here

Wandering the trout and dogwood forest
As our village is enlightened by the bombs;
Searching hooded for your silence, nest
Of last year's laying, the calm sad icon
Of your mouth. The children stay with nanna
In another place and year, my banished grace.

Having lived imprisoned in a hollow trunk
While winter soldiers barked and hunted work
You are here, cold beneath a shawl of leaves;
Your hair by now enwraps you like a cloak
Our tasteful furies tore away, muting the low
Music of the hooded man love half conceives.

IV

Romania

> *"Can't you see that in our country everything is silent? Nothing is moving, and nothing will ever move."*

(i)

From Palace Balconies

Cockroach moustaches. Script on talon.
Engraved on the band of a gift falcon
The Sultan sent his written permission
To the throne of my father in frost-bitten
Bucharest: we may celebrate again our Day
Of Independence in the traditional ways.
First I direct the planting of ranks of oaks
To enclose my orchards: here I will grow
Living towers of watchfulness, seed thickets
Of soldiers. *Stupid girl. No one shall exit.*
Then bitterly I will survey parades through the grey snow.

(ii)

Diplomats

Doubtless, it is a representative age.
They carry severed hands of our people
Into their meetings, hold them up in applause.
Canaries in shafts of antinomian
Histories of state, sensitive to plague,
They will never be permitted to die.

The diplomats are hard men, and nice men,
Jarred by nothing but fits of their loneliness,
Far from their children, searching for childish gifts;
Wise in the ventriloquist ways of the world.
Migratory, immured in the best of hotels,
Their wisdom is patiently binding their wrists.

Well read, they dream of the heart of the matter,
Where the ancient yet delicate art of *démarche*
And withdrawal has delivered itself to the waltz,
And where power—oh sweetest reverse!—serves
As an emblem for dance. Oh, they know better,
They always know better. Wherever they gaze
Pale floral paper subduing the halls:
Like an empire's desultory glance, this
Loneliness of evening in elegant hotels.

Even Tamurlaine had them, before and after rape.
Under the ferns, small mahogany tables
Sit by their knees in the bar, holding,
In spirit, their daughter's delicate dolls.

(iii)

Märchen

Two dented mannequins on snow and froth.
String of scarlet painted from the mouth.

*

Twenty-foot doorways, each carved oak door
Valued at a peasant's lifetime labour.
They'll do nicely. Two hundred on order.
Black bread scarce in the shops. Tea without sugar.

*

Deep in the *chei* of Carpathian beech
I found a chamoi tangled in the mist
By delicate horns flanged like a hammer's
Claw. Its bloody chestnut flanks were rent
By thorns. *Free me,* it wept, *I am innocent
And sacred.* I begged release. *Too late,* it hissed.
You must choose innocence or power.

*

We believed in the natural laws.
The queen was a doctor of economics.
We were as intimate with stakes and pyres
As a fifteenth-century bishop.

(iv)

1789, 1989

I

The panicking princes are neglecting their chains of command,
The Porte is forgetting its rapine and puppetry,
The crowns of Europe forget their fêtes for my father,
The counsellors salve the callouses capping their knees.
Amidst our spectacular guilt the citizens fathom their innocence
And polish the durable cobblestones under their feet.

My late father absorbed their bullets with the relishing force
      of their earlier cheers;
They are forgetting the flowers they flung from their throats.
One fool sings *The seam in society runs through our chests,*
But in Romania air of that grandest December hovered at freezing,
Snow turned to rain and the rain to ice and the ice flowed,
Meringues of slush recorded the hooves of the horses,
Parades returned to rebellion and the unified thousands
Spun with the skill of battalions, blind to their own gaze.

I cannot see they have altered their uniform aspect.
Amnesia's sweet cannibal lips! They are eating their keepsakes.

II

What will they make now of Wallachia and Moldavia
    the double kingdoms?
Forgetting they are separate threads, forgetting they are woven,
While delirious students recite in the rubble of squares
    All Europe is with us!
"The enemy of my enemy is my friend," so my father
    knelt knighted in London.

Out from the filigree light of the capital burning,
I've gone north into the oldest Moravian hamlets
    that even the Romans left whole;
Clusters of huts with gardens in front, their backs to the doors
    of the forest;
The woods, like a singular thought, free me to bury
The mouldering packets of father's most classical speeches:
"The source of all sovereignty essentially resides
    in the nation;
No group, no individual, may exercise authority
    not emanating therefrom."

III

There are moraines of snow through the upper valleys in spring,
And between the vine-laden laths of the village fences
And the first great beech graphing decades on sky,
A sudden March storm sweeps like forgotten regret,
Snow sifting here, and there, and further there, inscribing
    in the slight darkening
A third dimension of the air, my lingering eyes
    handling transparency.
The essential will of the nation remodels your kitchen
And rumples your bed.
Our Lord once wrote a word in the dirt with a stick, silently pointed,
    too cautious to speak.
The village priest who waits by my bedside tells me toward dawn
    he has always considered
        hypocrisy most likely.

(v)

Gargoyles

Fled, he for whom rebellion is not clarity
        But history unbound. Crowds swim, shadowy
As ideas. Under fog I've now forgone the city

And found this outer village aspect of my realm,
        Its aged infancy, crossing the frontiers that come
Between my shallow breaths, revoking home.

    marble gone slippery under blood

A pip of light in the woods. This kingdom of mud
        And smoke and gore was once my father's *tambal*, made
With a fine, stretched hide, played with the thud

Of little hammers, or, hard to see, the knobbed skulls
        Of flayed citizens that drummed in prison cells,
Ornamental.

(vi)

Open Skies

I

Here the cottages nest on sun-fluted paths
That open like chutes into the forest,

Hovering outside the tannic darkness
Like words afraid to enter a lover.

Here our mothers die, and distraught women
Who conceive of their hearts as an afterthought

(As humus to soil, as tears to water)
Send their too-meaningful stepdaughters

Down into the tangled stems and wild
With a handful of seeds to guide them;

Here the woodland rooks are ravenous,
And cringing creatures offer tests,

Exhausted rabbits shivering in snares
Present riddles with faces that stare

Lidless in two directions; and when the tale
Is complete you have mastered a lesson

That will never be applicable again.

II

In the capital the ministers of kings
Have convened to conclude how they might inspect
Each other's armies, enumerate soldiers
Numberless as the beech of Transylvania.
After the speeches they will gab like cousins
In plenary session, will assign inspectors
To survey the childish secrets of armies
Numberless as the beech of Transylvania.
The inspectors shall be blindfolded and scourged
And given handfuls of seeds where the houses
Are like words that long to enter a lover.
Perhaps you should mock them.
But they are crippled things where mothers die
And bitter parents send battered orphans
Down into the dreaming forests; after all
This is a morality tale with a lesson
That will never be applicable again.

(vii)

Ashputtle

She waltzed at the ball in a mask made of hide.
Her hair, over silk, had the texture of fur.
Her fingertips... At midnight she slipped from my side
And I bayed in chase through my kingdom's orchards of pear
(Stripped to send tribute to Turks). I foamed *True bride!*
Like a squirrel she skipped up into foliage. There
I had the tree felled. An empty sheaf. My soul's divide.

*

After the branch brushing a face on the road toward home,
After the axing of trees and the dovecote's burning,
After blood in the shoes, the sifting of ashes for bone,
Battalions of orphans—we talked at breakfast. "Spurning
Me twice—those beastly disguises—contempt for the throne
Of Moldavia. Some sort of test?" "Dear prince, still learning?
Don't find me familiar? I am simply the one
Who only if there seems a miracle in the meeting
Has truly been found." That night, again of course alone,

I crept through orchards ravaged of fruit. *You can't hide!*
I screamed, while the trees were collapsing like huts under pear-
Yellow moons. *Father's Romania is everywhere
And the tree's emptiness leaves this age deeply satisfied.*

V

Why I Need You

All the hotels in the world
Are the hotels of Minsk.
From their windows the statues
Are poets and slaughtermen
Put up in the parks
In identical poses, in the playing
Of children. There's no heat.
The radio plays one station
Called the voices of strangers.
It's always the middle of March.
The floorlady watches my door.
The restaurant closes
Before I am hungry.
All the women I do not love
Call to be exploited
For U.S. dollars only.
The mountains are flat.
The colours are slush.
There's no way to get warm.
My kids don't wake me
For glasses of water
In the middle of dreams.
The band in the bar plays *Feelings*.
The long distance line
Puts your voice in the room
And it almost seems real.
The shop in the lobby has cartons

Of Snickers, but no soap.
The hot water is cold.
Forget about breakfast.
This is how people live
After the divorce.
After all the wrong words,
After a hand cupping water
Goes gradually dry
There are the hotels of Minsk,
All the hotels in the world.

Ophelia Dreams of Akhmatova

Your whole life you have wanted
To stand as that woman, granted

Confusion by the lightly
Sketched-in tributary depths;

Darkly robed and nightly
Forgotten, the sky swept

By the occluding trees
Where much of the ink was spent,

Holding a little book,
A leather Pushkin, looking

Away,
The ferns leaning slowly

Waterward—and not as if
Waiting for some prison-emptying,

For an eventual freedom
Commensurate with a home—

The great will of unwaiting,
Your other hand against

A half-drawn willow tree,
A perfect frontispiece

That stands in place
Of each eventuality.

To T.M.

(a translation of "To S.E.," by Marina Tsvetaeva)

I have written on slabs of slate
And on filaments of faded fans,
And on riversand and on seasand,
On glass with a ring, on ice with a skate—

And on the bark of a hundred winters...
And finally, so everyone would know
That you are loved, loved, loved!
I wrote it all down—with the sky's rainbow.

For I longed that everyone flower
Down through centuries with me, under my fingers!
Later, my forehead bowed above the desk,
I crossed out a name, X after X.

But you, gripped in the faithless fists
Of the scribes! You who stung my heart raw
I will never turn in! Graven on the inside of the ring
You will endure in the tables of the law.

18 May 1920

Histories of Silence

      (i)

There, like a settling leaf, you have gone to sleep.
My quiet is a levity
                folded over and over unto density,
And how heavy it is and how it longs to be light.

I cannot speak to you of silence without freedom,
But those most fulsome in this matter are never free,
Sensing that the hilltop elm
Strands their nature in its unending silhouette,
As strange as all parts of memory
Unnoticed at the time and given now.
If I am free to tell you *this*, the lateral ruse
Outwitted, my love if I can use all "subtleties of speech,"
The slow leach of light beneath the bolted door—

Then I have changed the subject.
      I had wanted to tell you about my silence.

(ii)

The quietest grief is the grief on CNN,
Taking you live to the burning, the mother
On live feed from her home in Wichita
Telling us she is the mother of the child burning,
That she is learning live from her own TV
                (O my God, she says)
That it is hard to watch the burning, but she believes
We can learn something from this for the future.

Her word thing, the thing that goes and goes,
Pulls a suture through her body's throes, her lips,
(Not live, not coverage) and sews her mourning shut.

(Her telephone sits by the burning set.)

(iii)

Its unending silhouette.
In spring on the farm the runoff always found the cellar,
Easefully evading father's caulking, tarring, filler.
It crept up as I crept down the wooden steps,
A pearling edge of tension on the true-laid cement.
The furnace room was conquered to a quarter-inch,
Fathomless in dimness.

                I dreamt I found the board
That let the water in, and lifted it, shored
The cistern I discovered with my clever stones
And with an easy, sleepy, underwater breath
Kicked beneath the hurdle of the basement wall

        Into a running cavern without light or air,
Swimming down its curve to where the marshy bottom of the farm
Was sodden earth and silty water and roots of winter wheat.
I did not need to rise! or search a tracing back, I
                                could lie in wait,
Half hidden strainer of the weeds and water sinking through,
A membrane for the breathing of the field.

(iv)

The lateral ruse that fills the living rooms—
Yet somehow
         in the gloom of inner density I said
A levity is also folded down, and suffers us.

My aunt hidden there, her father calling *Catherine,
Catherine,* the day they came to take her from her home
To stay with kind relations while a widowed farmer,
With three such *little* girls, put himself to rights.
In the outhouse she held fast the inner latch,
Quiet,
     quiet and small while the ethereal voices
Waxed and waned in the beyond, holding shut the dark
With the shit smell in, crouched on the bum-worn seat.

How strong was she? How strong were they?
               How firmly could her lips . . .
If they could open the door her mother would be dead.

(v)

("Oduvanchik")

Breathe in and think about not yet breathing out.

A bravado cloud, a surge of chill and rain
Into a May Moscow day after weeks of heat

Scattering the walks I found of a country-ish lane
(Bending a stubborn medieval crook
Through the blocky, *prospekt*-riven *gorod*)
                         with fronds and poplar-down,
           the wet seed smell;

And past the Donskoi monastery's repainted walls,
                            white under gold
An unkempt garden of a ward for the insane
                 chock with dandelions

Reminded me that the Russian word
                for our *dents de lion*
Has "breath" or "blow" in the middle,
                           so I

Thought about a lovers' language where each thing is named
According to its midsummer future
                      lifted to the lips of a child.

October Again, Moscow

A hooded man in the aftermath of coups
And my very kindness overthrown. Pursued
Into the underpasses and across the squares
I found all lairs contracted and invaded, torn—
A concussion: like a heart or the frontal shells
Of blinded tanks. Thick seams beneath my creeping hands:
A quilted art, or else the sewn and resewn rags
Of a child I had long forgotten how to love.
Then a door, opening in, a line of cold
From ill-fitting panes, and a fallen curtain
Or shroud. Against my knee, certainly, a bed

With a pillow, or a sack of clothes to flee?
And the limbs still sleeping there, so that softly
Oh lord again how softly did my fingers care
On the cartography of hair, of lip, one
Curving collar bone, a flange of hip.
They found me here, my ear against the belly,
Listening to the looted statues of the city.

Notes to the Poems

Radiation — The phrases quoted in the first line of each poem are taken from *Betty Goodwin: Steel Notes* (National Gallery of Canada, 1989), as are other images and ideas in the suite.

Cover Their Faces — In memory of Karen.

Romania — The poem's epigraph is, I believe, from Vasile Milea. I have been unable to retrieve the precise source. Section two of "1789, 1989" concludes with lines from the Declaration of the Rights of Man passed by the French constituent assembly in August, 1789.

Histories of Silence — In part five, *prospekt* is the Russian for a major (straight, wide) street; *gorod* is the word for "city."

The translations of Bonnefoy are as faithful as I knew how to make them. They began as ways of trying to read him with greater attention and seemed to become part of my work. Other translations of these poems exist, and I do not pretend to better them, only to be satisfied for the moment with the pace and tone of those I reprint here. That of Phillippe Soupault's *Le Nageur* is "freer," but still, I think, a "translation." Those phrases rendered less literally result from attempts to "understand" the complex and disturbing images. My version of Marie-Claire Blais is a mongrel, most of it more or less literal, a few lines close to the original only in spirit (where literal renditions created, to my ear at least, dull English prose). Tsvetaeva's Russian is difficult to ungnarl at times even for Russians, but I have not (knowingly) altered the sense, while trying to salvage some of the poem's dense music, which simply cannot be reproduced in English.

ABOUT THE AUTHOR

Born and raised in rural Ontario, David Manicom lived in Toronto and then Montreal, where he obtained a PhD in literature from McGill and worked as an editor at the journal *Rubicon*. He now works in the Canadian foreign service. After postings in Russia and Pakistan, Manicom has recently returned to Canada, where he lives with his wife and three children in Aylmer, Quebec.

David Manicom's poetry has appeared in such publications as *Saturday Night, The Malahat Review, Shenandoah,* and *Descant*. His first collection, *Sense of Season,* (Porcepic, 1989) was followed by *Theology of Swallows* (Oolichan, 1991), which was shortlisted for the Lampman Award. A collection of short stories, *Ice in Dark Water,* will be published by Véhicule Press in 1997.